African Cookbook

Quick and Easy Recipes

with Authentic African Flavor

Includes both US and UK measurements and cooking terms

By

Minna Rose

LionheART Publishing House
Harrogate
UK

lionheartpublishinghouse@gmail.com

First published in Great Britain in 2015 by
LionheART Publishing House

ISBN: 978-1-912842-27-8
2nd edition

Contents

Introduction

Minna Rose enjoys traveling and loves to explore different cultures through food. She adds her own twists to the recipes she discovers and loves to share the results with her family and friends.

African food is vibrant, spicy and colorful, utilizing the most tantalizing flavors from the many cultures that have settled on the continent over the centuries, and creating new and wonderful combinations, combined with traditional foods and cooking methods.

Fresh and nutritious food is very important for a healthy life, just as tasty food, shared in good company, is essential for a happy and enjoyable life. Minna Rose's cookbooks combine the two in her recipes, all of which are easy to follow and recreate.

1. Lemon and Coriander Fish

Ingredients

2 white fish steaks or fillets (½ lb/250g)
Juice of 1 lemon
1 garlic clove – crushed (or 1 teaspoon of garlic paste)
1 teaspoon paprika
1 teaspoon ground coriander
Pinch salt and black pepper
1 tablespoon canola/rapeseed oil
1 red onion – sliced (approx. 1½ cups)
1 red chili – deseeded and chopped (approx. 1 teaspoon)
1 tablespoon fresh cilantro/coriander leaf - chopped

Serves 2

Marinate: 30 minutes

Preparation: 20 minutes

Serve with mashed yam (page 22) and kachumbali (page 26)

Preparation

1. Mix the lemon juice with the crushed garlic clove, paprika, ground coriander, salt and black pepper.
2. Rub this into the flesh of the fish, then leave to marinate for half an hour.
3. Heat the oil in a large skillet/frying pan. Add the fish (skin side down if using fillets).
4. Pour the rest of the marinade over the fish, add the red onion slices and red chili.
5. Turn the fish when cooked halfway through, and turn off the heat.
6. Add a handful of chopped fresh cilantro/coriander leaf.
7. Cover and allow the residual heat to cook through the rest of fish.
8. Serve with yam or mashed potatoes and kachumbali, or new potatoes and chili greens.

Using Up Leftovers

1. Mix the fish with diced red onion, chopped deseeded red chili, and mashed potato.
2. Put into a small, ovenproof dish and bake at 180°C/350°F/Gas mark 5 for approx. 10 minutes until heated through and the top is golden brown,
3. Serve with French fries and kachumbali.

2. Baked Mango and Turmeric Fish

Ingredients

2 whole fish such as trout or tilapia - cleaned
2 tablespoons/2oz/50g butter
4 green/spring onions – sliced (approx. ½ cup)
2 cloves garlic – crushed/minced (or 2 teaspoons garlic paste)
Juice of 1 lemon
1 red onion – diced (approx. 1 cup)
1 red bell pepper – deseeded and chopped (approx. 1 cup)
1 green chili – deseeded and diced (approx. 1 teaspoon)
1 x 15 oz/400g can diced/chopped tomatoes
1 ripe mango – diced
⅓ cup/100ml white wine
1 teaspoon turmeric
1 teaspoon dried thyme
1 teaspoon caster sugar
1 bouillon/stock cube (fish/chicken/vegetable)
1 tablespoon canola/rapeseed oil
Salt and black pepper
1 tablespoon fresh parsley – chopped

Serves 2

Marinate overnight

Preparation: 30 minutes

Serve with oven-baked potatoes

Preparation

1. Put the cleaned fish into a deep baking dish.

2. Squeeze the lemon juice over the fish, then sprinkle with dried thyme, 1 crushed/minced garlic clove, salt and black pepper and green/spring onions. Rub this mixture into both sides, and stuff the inside of the fish with the remainder.

3. Marinate overnight.

4. Dot the fish with small knobs of butter and bake at 180°C/350°F/gas mark 5 for 10 minutes, then turn and bake for a further 10 minutes while you prepare the sauce.

5. Fry the onion on a medium heat for approx. 5 minutes until soft. Add the crushed/minced garlic clove and diced chili, and stir.

6. Add the chopped red bell pepper, stir and cook 2 minutes.

7. Add the turmeric and sugar and stir.

8. Add the wine and chopped tomatoes and bring to the boil, stirring, for 2 minutes.

9. Crumble in the bouillon/stock cube and simmer for 5 minutes.

10. Pour the sauce over the fish, add the diced mango and replace in the oven for a further 10 minutes.

11. Sprinkle with chopped fresh parsley.

12. Serve with chili greens and yam, or on a bed of arugula/rocket with a baked potato.

Using Up Leftovers

Mix the fish and a small amount of sauce with mayonnaise and serve on oven-baked potato or in a sandwich.

3. African Spiced Turkey Leg

Serves 2

Preparation: 1-1½ hours

Serve with yam (page 22) and chakalaka (page 20)

This delicious way of cooking turkey was shared with me by a Zimbabwean friend and immediately became a favorite.

This recipe also works well with chicken.

Ingredients

2 small or 1 large turkey drumstick (1½ lb/700g)
2 tablespoons canola/rapeseed oil
1 tablespoon curry powder
1 tablespoon paprika
1 tablespoon garlic salt
1 tablespoon chicken gravy granules

Preparation

1. Press your fingers into the meat to feel for the groove between the muscles. Take a small sharp knife and cut down this groove lengthways.

2. Find the main bone with your knife and cut the meat away along the length of it to open up the drumstick(s) into a butterfly shape.

3. Sprinkle generously with oil and rub it in with your non-dominant hand.

4. Sprinkle on half the curry powder, paprika, garlic salt and gravy granules. Cup your non-dominant hand, fill with more oil and rub the marinade into the meat.

5. Turn the meat over and repeat to the other side.

6. Roast at 200°C/400°F/gas mark 6 for approximately 1-1½ hours, depending on size, until the meat is cooked, turning after half an hour, then every fifteen minutes.

7. Serve with chakalaka and African yam or mashed potato, veg and gravy or even fries/chips and salad.

Using Up Leftovers

1. Remove all the meat from the bone and roughly chop.
2. Slice one onion and fry.
3. Add a crushed garlic clove and half a chopped, deseeded red chili.
4. Stir.
5. Add a sliced red or yellow bell pepper.
6. Add the meat.
7. Stir and cook through.
8. Serve in wraps with sour cream. Add cheese if desired.

4. Lemon Chicken

Serves: 4
Preparation: 1½ hour
Serve with: mashed potato and roast vegetables

Ingredients

1 whole chicken – giblets removed (approx. 4lb/2kg)
2 tablespoons canola/rapeseed oil
2 chicken bouillon/stock cubes
2 lemons
1 red chili – finely chopped (approx. 1 teaspoon)
2 garlic cloves – crushed (or 2 teaspoons garlic paste)
6 green/spring onions – sliced (approx. ¾ cup)
1 red onion – sliced (approx. 1½ cups)
1 teaspoon dried thyme
1 teaspoon dried parsley

Preparation

1. First, spatchcock the chicken: Cut lengthways between the breasts, either side of the bone, with a sharp kitchen knife or strong kitchen scissors. Pull out the central bone then flatten out the meat.
2. Place the chicken in a deep, greased broiling/roasting tray, drizzle oil over both sides and rub it in.
3. Crumble a bouillon/stock cube over each side and rub this in.

4. Juice one lemon into a bowl & remove the pips. Add the chili, garlic, green/spring onions, thyme and parsley to the juice.
5. Mix well and spread half of this mixture over the chicken – meat-side up. Add half of the red onion slices plus slices of the second lemon.
6. Place the chicken in the oven, 200°C/400°F/gas mark 6 for 30 minutes

7. Turn the chicken, baste, and spread the rest of mixture, plus red onion and lemon slices over the skin. Return to the oven and cook for a further 30 minutes.
8. Turn again and baste after ¼ hour, and again after another 15 minutes or until the meat is cooked and juices run clear.
9. Serve with mashed potato and roast vegetables.

Using Up Leftovers

1. Put rice on to cook – adding a chicken bouillon/stock cube to the water for flavor.

2. Slice an onion, and gently fry it until soft (approx. 5 minutes). Add a deseeded and sliced green bell pepper, 1 crushed garlic clove, 1 red deseeded chili and fry for 1 minute.
3. Chop/shred the leftover chicken – add and stir.
4. Add the juice of ½ lemon, and a pinch of dried parsley and thyme,
5. Stir fry until the chicken is thoroughly warmed through.
6. Take off the heat, add 1 tablespoon of sour cream or crème fraiche. Mix well, return to the heat and simmer for 2 minutes.
7. Serve with the rice.

5. Chicken in Tomato, Spinach and Peanut Sauce

Ingredients

2 chicken breasts (approx. 10 oz/300g)
1 tablespoon canola/rapeseed oil
1 onion – diced (approx. 1 cup)
2 garlic cloves – crushed/minced (or 2 teaspoons garlic paste)
1 red chili – diced (approx. 1 teaspoon)
1 x 15 oz/400g can diced/chopped tomatoes
2 tablespoons smooth peanut butter
½ teaspoon dried thyme
2 chicken bouillon/stock cubes
Salt and black pepper
7 oz/200g fresh spinach

Serves: 2

Preparation: 20-30 minutes

Serve with: boiled yam (page 22)

Preparation

1. Fry the diced onion in a tablespoon of oil over a medium heat for approx. 5 minutes until soft.
2. Add the crushed/minced garlic and diced chili, and stir.
3. Slice the chicken breasts, add the meat to the pan and fry until browned.
4. Add the peanut butter and stir until melted and bubbling.
5. Add the can of tomatoes and thyme, and stir.
6. Crumble in the bouillon/stock cubes and add a pinch of salt and black pepper.
7. Simmer for 10 minutes or until the chicken is cooked through.
8. Tear the spinach, place on top of the cooking meat and sauce, and allow to wilt, then stir in – approx. 2 minutes

Using Up Leftovers

Can be chilled and reheated – ensure the chicken is heated through well before re-serving.

6. Tomato and Cumin Chicken

Ingredients

4 Chicken pieces (1½ lb/650g)
2-3 tablespoons canola/rapeseed oil
1-2 teaspoons cumin
1-2 teaspoons turmeric
1 x 6oz/164g tin or tube tomato paste/puree (1 cup)
3 cloves garlic – chopped (or 3 teaspoons garlic paste)
2 red and 1 green chilies – sliced (approx. 2 and 1 teaspoons)
1 x 15 oz/400g can diced/chopped tomatoes

Serves: 4

Preparation: approx. 1 hour

Serve with mashed potato or yam (page 22), and chakalaka (page 20)

Preparation

1. Place the chicken pieces in a deep, greased broiling tray or dish.
2. Drizzle half the canola/rapeseed oil over the chicken and rub in.
3. Sprinkle 1-2 teaspoons cumin and 1-2 teaspoons turmeric over the meat.
4. Spoon over half of the tomato paste/puree and rub it in.
5. Turn the chicken over and repeat.
6. Add the diced onion and sliced chili, plus the chopped/minced garlic.
7. Pour the can of tomatoes over the chicken.
8. Roast in the oven for 30 minutes at 200°C/400°F/gas mark 5.
9. Turn the chicken, spoon the excess sauce over top and cook for a further 30 minutes or until the chicken is cooked and juices run clear.

Using Up Leftovers

1. Chop an onion, garlic clove and deseeded, diced chili (or use leftover kachumbali) and fry in canola/rapeseed oil.
2. Add the diced, cooked chicken pieces, 1 teaspoon cumin and 1 teaspoon turmeric.
3. Stir well and add a can of diced/chopped tomatoes. Lower the heat and simmer for 5 minutes until the chicken is thoroughly heated through.

4. Take off the heat and add 1 tablespoon of sour cream, stir in, return to the heat and simmer for 2 minutes.
5. Serve with an oven-baked potato and salad.

7. Kebabs

Serves 2
Preparation: 20 minutes
Serve with raita, kachumbali and sautéed potatoes or yam

Ingredients

1 lb/450g ground chuck/minced beef
1 free-range egg
1 small red onion – diced (approx. 1 cup)
3 garlic cloves – crushed/minced (or 3 teaspoons garlic paste)
1 red chili – diced (approx. 1 teaspoon)
2 teaspoons fresh ginger - grated
2 teaspoons cumin
2 teaspoon ground coriander
2 teaspoon garam masala
Juice of ½ lemon (approx. 1 tablespoon)
2 slices bread – crumbed
Salt and black pepper
I tablespoon canola/rapeseed oil

Preparation

1. Put the meat, egg and spices in a bowl.
2. Dice the onion, and mince or crush the garlic, deseed and dice the chili and add to the bowl.
3. Squeeze in the juice of the half-lemon and mix well by hand.
4. Add the breadcrumbs and keep mixing until the mixture is firm.
5. Shape into balls about an inch in diameter (any larger and they are likely to break up when cooking).
6. For a more authentic kebab style, flatten into fingers and insert a wooden toothpick/cocktail stick or skewer into one end.
7. Heat the oil and fry the kebabs, turning, for 3-5 minutes until they are browned all over.
8. Drain well and serve with raita, kachumbali and sautéed potatoes or yam.

To make a Raita:

1. Peel and grate/shred ¼ English cucumber (about 4 oz/100g) and squeeze or press the excess moisture from it.
2. Place the cucumber flesh with ¼ cup/25g of mint, plus ¼ cup/25g of cilantro/coriander leaf, a green chili pepper, 1 tablespoon of lemon juice, 1 teaspoon of turmeric and 1 teaspoon of sugar into a small food processor and blitz
3. Stir this paste into 1 cup/250ml of Greek natural yoghurt.

Using Up Leftovers

Can be reheated in a curry sauce and served as kofta with naan, or with a tomato sauce for a milder flavor with pasta.

8. Spiced Lamb

Ingredients

1 lb/450g lamb pieces
1 red onion – diced (approx. 1 cup)
3 cloves garlic – minced/crushed (or 3 teaspoons garlic paste)
1 teaspoon fresh root ginger - grated
1-2 red chilies – deseeded and diced (approx. 2 teaspoons)
1 teaspoon paprika
1 teaspoon ground cinnamon
1 teaspoon ground cardamom
1 teaspoon dried basil
1 tablespoon canola/rapeseed oil
Salt and black pepper

Serves: 2

Preparation: 15 minutes

Serve with chili greens (page 24) and mashed potatoes

Preparation

1. Dice and fry the onion in a tablespoon of oil over a medium heat until soft – approx. 5 minutes.

2. Add the crushed/minced garlic and stir, cook for 1 -2 minutes.

3. Add the diced meat and fry, stirring well until it's browned.

4. Add the diced chili, grated ginger, spices and basil. Stir well.

5. Lower the heat and cook for 5-10 minutes until the meat is cooked through.

This recipe also works well with goat meat

Using Up Leftovers

1. Slice an onion and a deseeded red bell pepper, fry 5 minutes, then add the leftover meat.

2. Cook through and add more spices if required.

3. Serve in wraps with raita (page 15) and watercress, and French fries.

9. Goat Curry

Ingredients

2 lb/1 kg goat meat – cubed
2 red onions – diced (approx. 2 cups)
2 garlic cloves – minced/crushed (or 2 teaspoons garlic paste)
1 red bell pepper – deseeded and chopped (approx. 1 cup)
4 chilies – diced (approx. 4 teaspoons) – makes a medium-hot curry - adjust to own heat preference
2 beef bouillon/stock cubes
2 teaspoons turmeric
1 teaspoon cumin
1 teaspoon ground coriander
1 x 6oz/164g tin or tube tomato paste/puree (1 cup)
1 x 15 oz/400g can diced/chopped tomatoes
2 cups/500g natural yoghurt
1 teaspoon garam masala
1 handful chopped fresh cilantro/coriander leaf
1 teaspoon corn starch/cornflour
2 tablespoons canola/rapeseed oil

Serves: 4-6
Preparation: 2 – 2½ hours
Serve with: chili greens, naan and raita

Preparation

1. Fry the onion in two tablespoons of canola/rapeseed oil, in a large stock pot over a medium heat until soft – approx. 5 minutes.
2. Add the garlic and chili and stir well.
3. Add the dried spices and crumbled bouillon/stock cubes. Stir well.
4. Add the meat. Stir until browned – make sure to keep scraping the bottom of the pan to keep all that flavor.
5. Add the tomato paste/puree. Stir and cook for 1 minute.
6. Add the diced/chopped tomatoes. Stir, then lower the heat and simmer very gently for 1½ hours, stirring occasionally to allow the meat to tenderize and the spices to mellow.
7. Add the yoghurt and garam masala and stir well.
8. Simmer for a further 30 minutes.
9. Mix the corn starch/cornflour in a little cold water and add to the sauce to thicken if needed. Stir well and bubble through.
10. Add the chopped cilantro/coriander leaf.
11. Serve with chili greens or kachumbali, naan and raita.

To make a Raita:

1. Peel and grate/shred ¼ English cucumber (about 4 oz/100g) and squeeze or press the excess moisture from it.
2. Place the cucumber flesh with ¼ cup/25g of mint, plus ¼ cup/25g of cilantro/coriander leaf, a green chili pepper, 1 tablespoon of lemon juice, 1 teaspoon of turmeric and 1 teaspoon of sugar into a small food processor and blitz
3. Stir this paste into 1 cup/250ml of Greek natural yoghurt.

Using Up Leftovers

The curry can be frozen, then defrosted and thoroughly reheated to serve as above.

10. Chakalaka

A versatile and tasty vegetable dish use your favorite vegetables or use up leftovers from your fridge and/or freezer.

Ingredients

1 tablespoon canola/rapeseed oil
1 white onion – diced (approx. 1 cup)
2 cloves garlic – crushed/minced (or teaspoons garlic paste)
1 red chili – diced (approx. 1 teaspoon)
1 red bell pepper – deseeded and sliced (approx. 1 cup)
100g/4oz mixed vegetables [e.g. peas, carrot and (sweet)corn] (approx. 1 cup)
1 x 15 oz/400g can diced/chopped tomatoes

Seasoning
1 teaspoon paprika
1 teaspoon Worcestershire sauce
½ teaspoon mustard powder
Salt and black pepper

Serves: 2-4

Preparation: 10 minutes

Preparation

1. Dice and fry the onion in a tablespoon of oil for approx. 5 minutes until it's soft and turning brown.
2. Add the minced/crushed garlic and diced chili and fry 1 minute, stirring.
3. Add your diced veg – fresh and/or frozen.
4. Stir and cook 2 minutes.

5. Add the tin of diced/chopped tomatoes and seasoning.
6. Simmer for 2-5 minutes until thickened.
7. Serve with meat or fish dishes.

Using Up Leftovers

Can be reheated and served with a number of meat or fish dishes.

11. African Yam

Serves: 2

Preparation: 30 minutes

Take care not to confuse with cassava/manioc/yucca root, which looks very similar, but can be poisonous if not prepared properly.

Ingredients

1 small or ½ large yam
Boiling water
1 teaspoon salt

Preparation

1. Peel the yam and wash.
2. Chop into rough 1-inch-square pieces.
3. Place in a large saucepan, cover with water and add the salt. Bring to the boil and cook for 15-20 minutes until the yam is soft when pricked with a fork, and has a fluffy texture.
4. Drain and serve. Or it can be mashed with butter before serving.

Using Up Leftovers

1. Dice 1 red onion and a deseeded red chili.
2. Fry along with a crushed garlic clove in 1 tablespoon of canola/rapeseed oil.
3. Add your cooked yam pieces to the pan, along with slices of deseeded red bell pepper..
4. Fry until golden and heated through.
5. Serve with meat such as African spiced turkey leg (page 6).

12. Chili Greens

Ingredients

½ lb/200g spring greens/collard greens or kale
1 red onion – diced (approx. 1 cup)
1 red bell pepper – deseeded and sliced (approx. 1 cup)
1 green chili – diced (approx. 1 teaspoon)
3 garlic cloves – crushed/minced (or 3 teaspoons garlic paste
1 tablespoon canola/rapeseed oil
1″ fresh ginger – grated (approx. 1 tablespoon)
Salt and black pepper

Serves: 2-4

Preparation: 15 minutes

Preparation

1. Wash the greens, remove the stalks and cut out the 'spine' of the leaves.
2. Steam for 2 minutes until the leaves wilt, then place in a colander and allow to cool.
3. Squeeze any excess moisture out of the leaves then slice very thinly, and dice the chili, crush/mince the garlic and grate the ginger.
4. Fry the onion in oil until soft - approx. 5 minutes.
5. Add the chili, garlic, ginger and fry for 1 minute.
6. Add the greens and sliced red bell pepper, season with salt and black pepper and stir fry for 2 minutes until heated through.

Serve with cooked/roast meats, curries or fish.

13. Kachumbali

Ugandan Salad with a Kick!

Ingredients

1 red onion – diced (approx. 1 cup)
1 English cucumber – chopped (approx. 2 cups)
6 tomatoes – chopped (approx. 2 cups)
1 green chili – diced (approx. 1 teaspoon)
Juice of ½ lemon (approx. 1 tablespoon)
1 teaspoon salt

Serves: 2-4

Preparation: 10 minutes

Preparation

1. Dice the onion.
2. Slice the cucumber lengthways, cut into long sticks and roughly chop.
3. Roughly chop the tomatoes.
4. Finely chop the chili – if you prefer less heat, go for a larger red chili and deseed before chopping.
5. Mix all ingredients.
6. Add a teaspoon of salt and the juice of the half lemon.

Using Up Leftovers

If the salad is starting to get old, fry up with meat pieces and serve in wraps with sour cream.

14. Melon Orangilla

Ingredients

½ cantaloupe melon
½ honeydew melon
½ watermelon
1 orange
Juice of 1 lemon (approx. 2 tablespoons)

For the Orange Sauce
1¼ cup/300ml orange juice
1 tablespoon caster sugar
1 teaspoon vanilla extract
Grated rind of 1 orange

For the Vanilla Cream
1¼ cup/300ml heavy/whipping cream
3 teaspoons caster sugar
3 teaspoons vanilla extract

Serves: 2-4

Preparation: 30 minutes

Preparation

1. Firstly prepare the orange sauce by pouring the orange juice into a small pan.
2. Add the sugar and bring to the boil.
3. Lower the heat and simmer for approx. 20 minutes to thicken into a syrup.
4. Allow to cool, then stir in the vanilla extract.
5. In a bowl, cube the melon and squeeze the lemon juice over the fruit. Mix to coat.
6. Whip the cream, adding 3 teaspoons of caster sugar and vanilla extract.
7. Place the melon on plates, along with some orange segments add a serving of vanilla cream to each, and spoon some orange sauce over the top to serve.

Use up extra melon by mixing with slices of kiwifruit/Chinese gooseberry and orange segments to make a tropical fruit salad.

15. Tropical Crêpes

Ingredients

1¼ cups/125g self-rising flour
1 tablespoon caster sugar
2 free-range eggs
1¼ cup/300ml milk
Pinch nutmeg
1-2 tablespoons/1-2 oz/25-50g butter
A mixture of tropical fruit, e.g:
1 orange (or satsuma or nectarine)
1 kiwi fruit
1 mango
1 papaya

Serves: 1-4

Preparation: 10-15 minutes

Serve with: vanilla ice-cream or whipped cream.

Preparation

1. Prepare the fruit by skinning if needed and slicing.
2. Sift the flour into a bowl, crack in the eggs, add the sugar and nutmeg and ¼ cup/50ml of the milk.
3. Whisk to combine (either by hand or with a food processor).
4. Continue to beat as you slowly add more milk until you get the consistency of heavy/double cream, which coats the back of a spoon.
5. Heat a knob of butter in a small skillet/frying pan.
6. Pour in enough batter to thinly coat the base of the pan and cook for approx. 30 seconds. Use a spatula to check that the bottom is golden brown.
7. Flip – either with the spatula or by tossing – then cook for a further 30 seconds.

About the Author

Minna Rose is the Chronic Cook.

She has battled chronic pain and fatigue for twenty-five years, since a diagnosis of fibromyalgia. She is determined to live her life as fully—and independently—as possible, which includes cooking healthy meals in her own kitchen. From the initial reaction of, "I can't do that anymore," she changed her thinking to: "Maybe there's a way I can . . ."

www.minnarose.com

The Chronic Cook Facebook Page:
www.facebook.com/thechroniccook

The Chronic Kitchen Facebook Group:
www.facebook.com/groups/chronickitchen

Instagram: @chronic_cooking

Twitter: @minnarosecooks

Email: minnarose2015@gmail.com

Books by Minna Rose

KITCHEN CULINARY DICTIONARY: American/British

UTTERLY BUTTERY COOKBOOK: Impress with flavoured butters for dinner parties, family dinners, barbecues, and quick and easy meals.

LOW-OXALATE COOKBOOK: Osteoporosis, Fibromyalgia, Kidney Stones

IMMUNE-BOOSTING COOKBOOK: Supporting your Immune System through Diet

GERMAN COOKBOOK: Delicious, Traditional Recipes with Authentic German Flavour

AFRICAN COOKBOOK: Quick and Easy Recipes with Authentic Flavour

www.minnarose.com

Printed in Dunstable, United Kingdom

64679663R00022